MW01125245

Authority Issues

....

When It's Hard Being Told
What to Do

Robert Smith

New
Growth
Press
www.newgrowthpress.com

New Growth Press, Greensboro, NC 27404
www.newgrowthpress.com

Cover Design: Tandem Creative, Tom Temple,
tandemcreative.net

Typesetting: Lisa Parnell, lparnell.com

ISBN-10: 1-936768-39-9
ISBN-13: 978-1-936768-39-4

Library of Congress Cataloging-in-Publication Data
Smith, Robert
 Authority issues : when it's hard being told what to do / Robert Smith.
    p. cm.
 Includes bibliographical references and index.
 ISBN-13: 978-1-936768-39-4 (alk. paper)
 ISBN-10: 1-936768-39-9 (alk. paper)
 1. Authority—Biblical teaching. 2. Authority—Religious aspects—
Christianity. I. Title.
 BS680.A93S65 2011
 262'.8—dc23
                                                      2011038274

Printed in Canada
21 20 19 18 17 16 15 14   4 5 6 7 8

My Platoon Sergeant did it—again! We were done with the day's training at 1400. I thought we would go home early, but we had to stick around until the closeout formation at 1645 "just in case" something came up. Why do we have an alert roster? He could activate it so we could get all the information that was put out. With deployment coming up, it would really be nice to hang out a little before we go "over there" again.

Have you ever had a day like that? Or a time like the following:

> He did it again! How does he expect me to make this work when he keeps changing his mind about what he wants? Last week he insisted that we complete this procedure in seven minutes. Today, he raked me over the coals in staff meeting because the procedure wasn't thorough enough. He said he thought it was obvious that a seven-minute procedure wasn't enough time to get the results we need. Once again, I'm made to look like an idiot for following his instructions!

Most of us have been there. It may not have been a seven-minute procedure or a late dismissal that was the issue, but we know what it's like to be under authority that fails. It's hard!

When we were kids, the authorities that failed were usually our parents or teachers. Now that we've grown up, it turns out that our boss (or drill sergeant or commanding officer or even our chaplain or pastor) seems to have taken lessons from the people we had to obey as kids. Did they all go to the same leadership school or what? In addition to that, we have the little frustrations that pop up day-to-day. Yesterday the construction flag person made us wait ten minutes while she gave the right-of-way to traffic in the opposite direction. Even when there weren't any cars coming she stood there holding her stop sign and chatting with her buddies. Why can't she get a clue?!

There are many reasons not to submit to imperfect authority, aren't there?

- The authority is unreasonable.
- The authority is wrong.
- The authority doesn't understand.
- The leadership is inconsistent.
- Doing it the boss's way will lead to failure.
- Submitting will ruin my schedule.
- The authority doesn't practice what he preaches; he has no integrity.
- The authority is unqualified; I respect the rank, but not the person.
- The authority acts like a dictator.

This negative reasoning inevitably leads to actions like the following:

- Feeling sorry for myself
- Focusing on my "right" to be treated better
- Gossiping (sometimes in the guise of a prayer request)
- Complaining
- Getting others to agree with me, gaining a following
- Offering token submission—just enough to get by and avoid serious consequences

- Withdrawing
- Becoming bitter
- Just plain resisting
- Ignoring instructions
- Getting angry
- Arguing
- Getting even
- Doing it my way

It's easy to submit when our authority does what we like. When the Command Sergeant Major walks the Battalion and Company areas to make sure we are released on time for Family Day, we're fine. When we're the teacher's pet or the hand-picked successor, submission doesn't seem hard. When our boss gives us our second raise in six months, when our husband brings us flowers and takes over the kids' bedtime routine, when our pastor is in complete agreement about supporting the missionary we've suggested, and when the government lowers our taxes, life is good!

However, when an authority you applaud is replaced with an authority who does something you consider wrong, an authority who makes a decision you seriously question, or an authority who communicates in an unpleasant manner, suddenly it's not easy. When you work for an authority who requires an action that is inconvenient for you, who falsely accuses you, or who makes poor decisions, life gets hard. What happened?

The bottom-line answer to that question is that no human authority will ever be perfect. Since the time Adam and Eve chose not to trust God or submit to him in the

Garden of Eden, the world has been broken by sin. The problems sin causes show up everywhere, every day, including in our leaders.

But what if we were under perfect authority? Sadly, it's not just those in authority who are broken by sin; we are too. That means we would fail in the way we submitted even to authorities who never made a mistake. Don't think so? Consider Adam and Eve's situation: God was their Creator and Father. He had given them a perfect home, perfect bodies, a great job of being in charge of the whole creation, and just one little rule: "You may surely eat of every tree of the garden, but of the tree of the knowledge of good and evil you shall not eat, for in the day that you eat of it you shall surely die" (Genesis 2:16–17). Despite a perfect life with perfect authority, Adam and Eve still disobeyed. It is easy to think we could solve our problems with authority if we could change those who are in authority, but the story of Adam and Eve shows us that our problems with authority go deeper than what others are doing. Our problem stems from what's in our hearts.

Adam and Eve needed help from outside themselves. Their failure to submit filled the world with brokenness, pain, and death, but God promised Adam and Eve that he would send Someone to save them. The Savior would submit perfectly and then give his life as a payment not just for Adam and Eve's sins, but the sins of all who come to him in faith. The Savior is Jesus, God's own Son. This minibook will explain God's view of submission, and how coming to him in faith will give you the power to submit wisely, even when it's hard or feels impossible.

God's View of Submission

No one can escape submitting to authority! Each of us is required by God to submit to someone. Children are to obey parents (Ephesians 6:1–3). Wives are to submit to husbands (Ephesians 5:22; 1 Peter 3:1). Church members are to submit to pastors (1 Corinthians 16:15–16; Hebrews 13:17). Employees are to submit to employers (Ephesians 6:5; Colossians 3:22; 1 Peter 2:18). Everyone is to submit to the government (Romans 13:1–5; 1 Peter 2:13–14). All believers are to submit to each other (Ephesians 5:21; 1 Peter 5:5) and to God (Romans 6:13; James 4:7).

Biblical Submission

Submission is defined as voluntarily placing oneself under the authority of a leader. It is a military term describing the relationship of a soldier to an officer. Submission means to subordinate or subject oneself to the authority. Those who submit recognize and honor the authority held by the one placed over them.

Submission is a choice; it is an act of the will. Submission is not to be offered "reluctantly as the defeated general submits to his conqueror, but voluntarily as the patient on the operating table submits to the skilled hand of the surgeon as he wields his knife."[1]

Submission Is the Believer's Required Way of Life

Jesus modeled submission for us in his relationship to the Father. He said in John 6:38, "For I have come down from heaven, not to do my own will but the will of him who sent me." In John 8:29, he said, "And he who sent me is with me. He has not left me alone, for I always do the things that are pleasing to him."

Since submission was the way of life for Christ, it is to be the way of life for all believers. Romans 8:28–29 teaches that all we experience in life is intended to make us more like Christ, which includes learning his kind of submission.

We need to learn more about Jesus' submission to learn how it is possible for us to follow his example. Remember that since Adam and Eve lived we have all been broken by sin (Romans 3:23). If we were required to pay for our own sins, we would all be bound for death and an eternity in hell, separated from God forever (Romans 6:23). But God loves us so much that he sent Jesus to earth to live a perfect life for us and to then die in our place. Since Jesus never sinned, he did not need to die for his own sins. Thus, his death is acceptable to God as a substitute payment for our sins (John 3:16). All we need to do is personally accept that payment on our behalf (Romans 10:9–10).

God's plan to save his people was based on Jesus voluntarily going to the cross. Jesus' love for us is seen in his submission to his Father's plan. This changed everything for us, including the context in which *we* submit to authority. Jesus defeated sin *in* us and *against* us. He enables us to do what is right and protects us from being defeated by evil. All this happens because he submitted to unjust human authority—*because* he submitted to the divine authority who was behind it and would overrule it. In short, Christ submitted to unjust authority *because* he was submitting to his Father. Human authorities did not have the last word; God did (John 19:11; Acts 2:23). Jesus' death on our behalf is the proof and ultimate example of God's ability to work good through evil. That is the perspective we need as we face the authorities in our lives. Anyone who doubts that God can work good through evil only needs to look at the cross. God calls Christ's followers to allow him to work in our lives in similar ways. He calls us to trust and submit to him before we do the same with human authority.

Submission Is Required Even When Authority Fails

As we saw earlier, because of the curse of sin we can expect all authority to fail. What provision has God made when this failure is harsh or unjust or unreasonable or unpleasant? Are we excused from submission? Should we lead a mutiny? No, submission is required even to authority that fails in those ways.

For example, the husband referred to in 1 Peter is unsaved and does not obey God's Word, but submission is still required. "Likewise, wives, be subject to your own husbands, so that even if some do not obey the word, they may be won without a word by the conduct of their wives" (1 Peter 3:1). If the husband is saved but does not obey God's Word, the principle is the same.

The master also referred to in 1 Peter is harsh or unreasonable, but God still requires submission.[2] "Servants, be subject to your masters with all respect, not only to the good and gentle but also to the unjust" (1 Peter 2:18). The governing authority at the time Paul wrote Romans was Nero—an incredibly cruel emperor—but submission was still required.

> Let every person be subject to the governing
> authorities. For there is no authority except from

God, and those that exist have been instituted by God. Therefore whoever resists the authorities resists what God has appointed, and those who resist will incur judgment. (Romans 13:1–2)

According to Paul, resisting authority is dangerous because it is actually resisting God. When you criticize the authority, you are criticizing the God who placed that leadership over you. You are deliberately taking a dangerous position.

Having said this, it's important to note that no human authority is given all of God's authority. Each leader is given very limited authority, clearly defined by God in the Bible. No leader has the authority to ask another person to sin. Therefore, if you are asked to sin, you should respectfully refuse to submit.

In addition, no military leader is given unlimited authority, but is responsible to his or her superior officers for the way in which his duties are performed. If your leader is abusing authority, pursuing the matter through appropriate channels is a legitimate way to be submissive to the chain of command as a whole. Similarly, the leadership a husband exercises in the home should reflect his submission to his spiritual leaders. If he is abusive in the way he leads his wife and family, the family can legitimately ask for the help of the leaders of the church and, if needed, law enforcement.

How to Change the Way You Think

Those in authority often make life very difficult. What should you do when it seems that wrong or unjust decisions are being made? What can you do instead of resisting, complaining, or becoming bitter and angry?

Go to God with Your Struggles and Questions

Even God's prophets struggled with how to respond well to authority. In the Old Testament, the prophet Habakkuk could not understand the decisions of the authority over him. That's not surprising perhaps—until you realize that Habakkuk's authority was God. But Habakkuk does not turn away from God; instead, he goes straight to him with his questions and struggles.

> The oracle that Habakkuk the prophet saw.
> O Lord, how long shall I cry for help,
>   and you will not hear?
> Or cry to you "Violence!"
>   and you will not save?
> Why do you make me see iniquity,
>   and why do you idly look at wrong?
> Destruction and violence are before me;
>   strife and contention arise.
> So the law is paralyzed,
>   and justice never goes forth.
> For the wicked surround the righteous;
>   so justice goes forth perverted. (Habakkuk 1:1–4)

God doesn't turn from Habakkuk in disgust. Instead he answers Habakkuk.

> "Look among the nations, and see;
>   wonder and be astounded.

For I am doing a work in your days
  that you would not believe if told."
(Habakkuk 1:5)

God tells Habakkuk he is sending the Chaldeans to ensure that Israel's evil will not continue unpunished. And the end result was that God would be glorified through these events: "But the LORD is in his holy temple; let all the earth keep silence before him" (Habakkuk 2:20). Habakkuk learns that God is in control and that he needs to trust him even when he doesn't understand what God is doing or why he is doing it. God uses all human authority to accomplish his purposes. That truth applies now as much as it did then. Even though to our logic authorities may seem unreasonable, God is in control. He has a plan that glorifies himself and is best for his people.

If you are in a difficult situation like Habakkuk, you can go to God with your questions and your struggles. He will hear you and help you. Perhaps as you read on through this minibook, you will hear some of God's answers for you in your struggles with authority. Many believers have no answers or hope for people in situations that are hard to understand. But God wants us to realize that he is in control even then. Let's take a closer look at what God says about these issues.

Remember That God Is in Control

"The king's heart is a stream of water in the hand of the LORD; he turns it wherever he will" (Proverbs 21:1). Remember that just because your leader makes a decision that is unpleasant to you, God did not suddenly lose

Robert Smith

control. If God has control over the king's heart, he has control over your situation even when your leader fails.

Ask yourself, "Could God have prevented this situation?" The answer is obviously yes. So why didn't he? There may be many reasons. One of them may be that God wants to teach you to recognize his sovereign control. He may want to increase your skill in seeing his control in all things.

You can choose to believe God is in control since he said he is. Believing God is in control when it doesn't make sense to you becomes an opportunity to trust God. You have a choice. You may choose to believe God and his Word, or you may choose to trust your logic or experience. Jerry Bridges states, "God will never allow any action against you that is not in accord with his will for you. And his will is always directed to your good."[3]

Recognize That God Can Use the Leader's Failures for Your Good and His Glory

> And we know that God causes all things to
> work together for good to those who love
> God, to those who are called according to *His*
> purpose. For those whom He foreknew, He also
> predestined to *become* conformed to the image
> of His Son, so that He would be the firstborn
> among many brethren. (Romans 8:28–29 NASB,
> emphasis added)

> As for you, you meant evil against me, but God
> meant it for good, to bring it about that many
> people should be kept alive, as they are today.
> (Genesis 50:20)

What seems like a mistake to you is really God at work to accomplish what he desires in your life. Jerry Bridges reminds us, "Neither the willful malicious acts nor the unintended mistakes of people can thwart God's purpose for us."[4] God is always ultimately doing something good, and that good far outweighs the discomfort caused by the failure. "God never pursues his glory at the expense of the good of his people, nor does he ever seek our good at the expense of his glory. He has designed his eternal purpose so that his glory and our good are inextricably bound together."[5]

Recognize That the Difficulty Will Not Be Too Much

> No temptation has overtaken you that is not common to man. God is faithful, and he will not let you be tempted beyond your ability, but with the temptation he will also provide the way of escape, that you may be able to endure it. (1 Corinthians 10:13)

Even when your authority fails, God will never require you to deal with more than you can handle. He will never allow a trial that will cause you to respond sinfully. He wants you to grow under that leadership. He will help you to bear up under it. He has provided a way of escape and a light at the end of the tunnel. He is encouraging you to stand strong in the trial, to persevere, and to use it to please him because he promises that it will ultimately end. (Note: According to this verse, the way of escape is not to escape but to endure.)

Thank God for Everything, Including the Leadership over You

"Giving thanks always and for everything to God the Father in the name of our Lord Jesus Christ" (Ephesians 5:20). God put that leader over you as a part of his good plan for you. Consider the benefits listed above and thank God for them. This helps you to see that this authority is really a gift from God to you. Thanksgiving makes it easier to have the right attitude toward your authority. It keeps you from becoming bitter for her failures and it helps you focus on your leader's good qualities.

Place Your Trust in God, Not the Authority

Habakkuk trusted in God. He decided to trust God even if it didn't make sense to him. As he writes in Habakkuk 3:17–19,

> Though the fig tree should not blossom, nor fruit be on the vines, the produce of the olive fail and the fields yield no food, the flock be cut off from the fold and there be no herd in the stalls, yet I will rejoice in the LORD; I will take joy in the God of my salvation. GOD, the Lord, is my strength; he makes my feet like the deer's; he makes me tread on my high places.

Depend on God's Grace to Help

Second Corinthians 9:8 says, "And God is able to make all grace abound to you, so that in all things at all times, having all that you need, you will abound in every good work" (NIV). God has promised his grace for all your needs, therefore, you can bear up under your authority by God's grace. You can grow as God desires by his grace.

How to Change the Way You Act

Be an Example of a Godly Response

Christ set the example he wants—and enables—you to follow.

> Your attitude should be the same as that of Christ Jesus. (Philippians 2:5 NIV)

> For to this you have been called, because Christ also suffered for you, leaving you an example, so that you might follow in his steps. (1 Peter 2:21)

> Whoever claims to live in him must walk as Jesus did. (1 John 2:6 NIV)

If you do not have the right attitude toward authority in your life, you won't have a message of hope for those under your leadership in your team or section. The husband who doesn't properly respond to the failures of his boss has no ministry to his family, who lives under *his* failing leadership. He is basically saying, "Do as I tell you, not do as I do. My example is not important." In the same way, the wife who doesn't respond in a godly way to the failures of her husband will have no ministry to her children who live under *her* failing leadership.

Similarly, the deacon or elder who resists the decisions of the church (which includes the pastor, board of elders, or congregation) loses his ministry. When he resists decisions made by the church, crusades for his position, or quietly foments opposition, he negates his ministry.

Those under authority who do not enthusiastically submit to the authority God has placed over them are not submitting to God. They are functioning as though there are occasions when a person may reject God's authority. They should not be surprised, then, when those under their authority follow their example by resisting them.

Pray for Those in Authority over You

First of all, then, I urge that supplications, prayers, intercessions, and thanksgivings be made for all people, for kings and all who are in high positions, that we may lead a peaceful and quiet life, godly and dignified in every way. (1 Timothy 2:1–2)

Pray for the salvation of your leaders if they are not saved. Pray for their growth in the character of Christ if they are. Ask God to help your leaders in their responsibilities so that they will be successful in their positions. Pray that God will use your authorities' decisions to his glory and that you will respond to them as God desires. Pray that God would use you to help make your authorities successful.

Pray that God would help your authorities to handle the pressures that come with their position, and ask God to bless them. Finally, thank God that he has placed your authorities over you. Thank him for the opportunities he is giving you for growth.

Honor Those in Authority Because of Their Position

> Honor everyone. Love the brotherhood. Fear God. Honor the emperor. (1 Peter 2:17)

> Let as many bondservants as are under the yoke count their own masters worthy of all honor, so that the name of God and His doctrine may not be blasphemed. And those who have believing masters, let them not despise them because they are brethren, but rather serve them because those who are benefited are believers and beloved. Teach and exhort these things. (1 Timothy 6:1–2 NKJV)

Remember that God is the One who appointed your authorities. God commands you to honor them.

Honor them by speaking to them respectfully and by supporting them to others. Honor them by refusing to listen to others tear them down. Honor them by working wholeheartedly to accomplish their goals. Honor them by following their instructions completely.

Honoring your authorities prevents discredit to God's name. Honoring them is especially important if you have Christian leaders, because those who benefit from their leadership are your brothers and sisters in Christ, your loved and dear friends.

Concentrate on Your Responsibility

> Why do you see the speck that is in your brother's eye, but do not notice the log that is in your own

eye? Or how can you say to your brother, "Let
me take the speck out of your eye," when there is
the log in your own eye? You hypocrite, first take
the log out of your own eye, and then you will see
clearly to take the speck out of your brother's eye.
(Matthew 7:3–5)

Therefore you have no excuse, O man, every one
of you who judges. For in passing judgment on
another you condemn yourself, because you, the
judge, practice the very same things. (Romans 2:1)

Remember, you sin too. If you were the leader, you
would not be perfect either. Think about how you would
like to be treated in a leadership position.

It is true that your authorities are accountable for
their leadership, but if their accountability is your main
emphasis, you are violating Matthew 7:3–5. You are more
concerned about your authorities' responsibility than your
own. You are concentrating more on your authorities' relationship to God than on your relationship to God and the
leaders he has placed over you. You must focus more on
your accountability than on changing your authority.

You may have been part of a church where you observed
members who were more concerned about the failures of
their leaders than their own responsibility. Ignoring their
own sin, these Christians were more concerned about the
pastor doing his job than they were about fulfilling their
own responsibilities. Christians like this keep church leadership under a magnifying glass, ready to confront them
about every little thing.

These Christians often go from church to church because they are only concerned about what God says to the pastor and how the pastor is to be accountable. They are not concerned about what God requires of them. They don't listen to sound doctrine about Christian growth because they are more interested in checking up on the pastor than they are about their own growth in Christlikeness.

Remember, each failure by a leader has the specific purpose of developing the character of Christ in you. God is up to something good. You pray, "Lord, help me grow." Many times the Lord answers by revealing and using failure in your leaders.

Often the quality God wants to develop in you will be directly related to the failure you see in the authority. To repeat Romans 2:1, "Therefore you have no excuse, O man, every one of you who judges. For in passing judgment on another you condemn yourself, because you, the judge, practice the very same things." If the boss blows up at you, maybe God wants you to see that you are having trouble dealing with your anger. If the pastor seems to expect too much of you, maybe God wants you to be more realistic in your expectations of your family. When your authority does something you don't like, look at it through the lens of Romans 2:1 and see what might need to be changed in your life.

Let me use an example that most military people will recognize. During basic training a new recruit experiences what seems like useless torture as he is required to submit to a drill sergeant who seems to have no mercy. He must eat so rapidly his mother would be upset because he didn't chew his food. He works under sleep-deprived conditions. He is restricted in what he can say and when he can say it. He learns to follow the drill sergeant even when it seems the most foolish thing he can do. His body is sore, tired, and hungry. At that point, he can become distressed with his circumstances and fail to see the big picture behind them. When he realizes that the drill sergeant is doing his best to simulate battle conditions without the dangers of bullets, he will be grateful for what he is learning. He will focus on his responsibility to learn all he can so that when the real battle comes, his mind is free to focus on combat. In the middle of a real battle he will reflect, with gratitude, on the training provided by the drill sergeant.

Respond as Christ Did

> For to this you have been called, because Christ
> also suffered for you, leaving you an example,
> so that you might follow in his steps. He
> committed no sin, neither was deceit found in
> his mouth. When he was reviled, he did not
> revile in return; when he suffered, he did not
> threaten, but continued entrusting himself to
> him who judges justly. (1 Peter 2:21–23)

It is not to your credit to respond sinfully when leadership fails. Anyone can respond that way. Only when you respond as Christ did are you pleasing God. Even when you are convinced you are right and the authority is wrong, you are still to respond according to biblical principles. Christ responded sinlessly to the human authority that

failed in his life *because* of his submission to his Father.
You can respond properly to human authority because, by
the power of the Holy Spirit, you can follow the example
of Christ (1 Peter 2:21). Your confidence in Christ's work
on your behalf enables you to submit to authority by faith,
making you more like Christ.

And as you respond in obedience and faith, remember
that Jesus understands the struggle and is praying for you.

> We do not have a high priest who is unable to
> sympathize with our weaknesses, but one who
> in every respect has been tempted as we are, yet
> without sin. Let us then with confidence draw
> near to the throne of grace, that we may receive
> mercy and find grace to help in time of need.
> (Hebrews 4:15–16)

Return Good for Evil

Romans 12:21 says, "Do not be overcome by evil, but
overcome evil with good."

The natural tendency for us is to return evil for evil
because we want to get even. However, this response doesn't
produce anything but more evil. God says to put away that
"little pop gun." Instead, use the "atomic weapon" he pre-
scribes. God says to return good for evil.

Some complain, "But returning good for evil condones
the bad done to me." It is not up to you to be your authority's conscience. It is the Holy Spirit's work to convict of
sin, not yours. Don't try to do God's job for him. You will
mess it up because you are violating his Word.

Others complain, "But it isn't natural to return good for evil." True! We have responded sinfully so often that sinful responses are natural habits. Nevertheless, we are to do what God says, not what is natural. At first, responding biblically will not feel natural. Anything you do at first is awkward. Only by choosing right responses over and over does responding properly become natural. If you have responded sinfully, you need to repent and confess the sin. Then, through the power of the indwelling Holy Spirit, do what God says so often that obeying him becomes what you more naturally choose to do.

Responding properly requires planning ahead. Plan the right action to prevent an automatic sinful action. The first step is to pray for your authorities since they are God's choice for you. When your leader is doing a poor job, work on helping him rather than criticizing him.

If you speak to your authority about any concerns, be sure to follow biblical principles. Speak in love to solve problems instead of trying to get your own way. Learn how you can help your leader. Concentrate on ways to help her succeed in her role, rather than working on how to get rid of her. Remember that returning good for evil never requires that you do something ungodly or sinful. In fact, returning good for evil to those in authority over you can mean saying no when you are asked to do something that God says is wrong.

The biblical answer to an authority who fails is a godly response; it is not to try to show the leader how she is wrong or to try to get her to change. Instead, use the failure of your authority to become more like Christ, which will prevent bitterness, produce good fruit in you, and prevent living to change your leaders.

Action Steps:

- List sinful ways you tend to respond to authority who fails (e.g., I complain to my spouse; I harbor resentment; I waste time on the job fretting about my authority).
- Ask forgiveness from God and those affected by your past failures.
- List fifteen ways your authority provides good leadership.
- Pray daily, thanking God for your authority and asking him to help you see the log in your own eye.
- Review Romans 8:28–29 twenty-five times each day for a week.
- Daily list three ways you applied Romans 8:28–29 to your situation.

Endnotes

1. Jerry Bridges, *Trusting God* (Colorado Springs, Colo.: NavPress, 1988), 177.

2. The word "harsh" is also translated "unreasonable" (NASB), "cruel" (Christian Counselors New Testament), and "surly, overbearing, unjust, or crooked" (Amplified).

3. Bridges, *Trusting God*, 71.

4. Ibid., 40.

5. Ibid., 25–26.